emptied

JAIME CROWE

STONE & SKY
PRESS

For the forgotten selves
we exiled to survive.

For the wonder, wildness, softness, and inner knowing
we were taught to silence.

Come back.
It is time.

EASTER 2026

I finished my first book.
I don't think it's a coincidence.
I don't believe in those.

I said, "It is finished."
And I began to cry.

The words of an ending,
at the threshold of something new.

Emptied.

On the day that is about what comes after the worst thing.

The tomb being empty.
The beauty of renewal.
The pain we must endure.
The questioning.
The waiting.
The grief.
The emptying of everything that came before.

I wept.

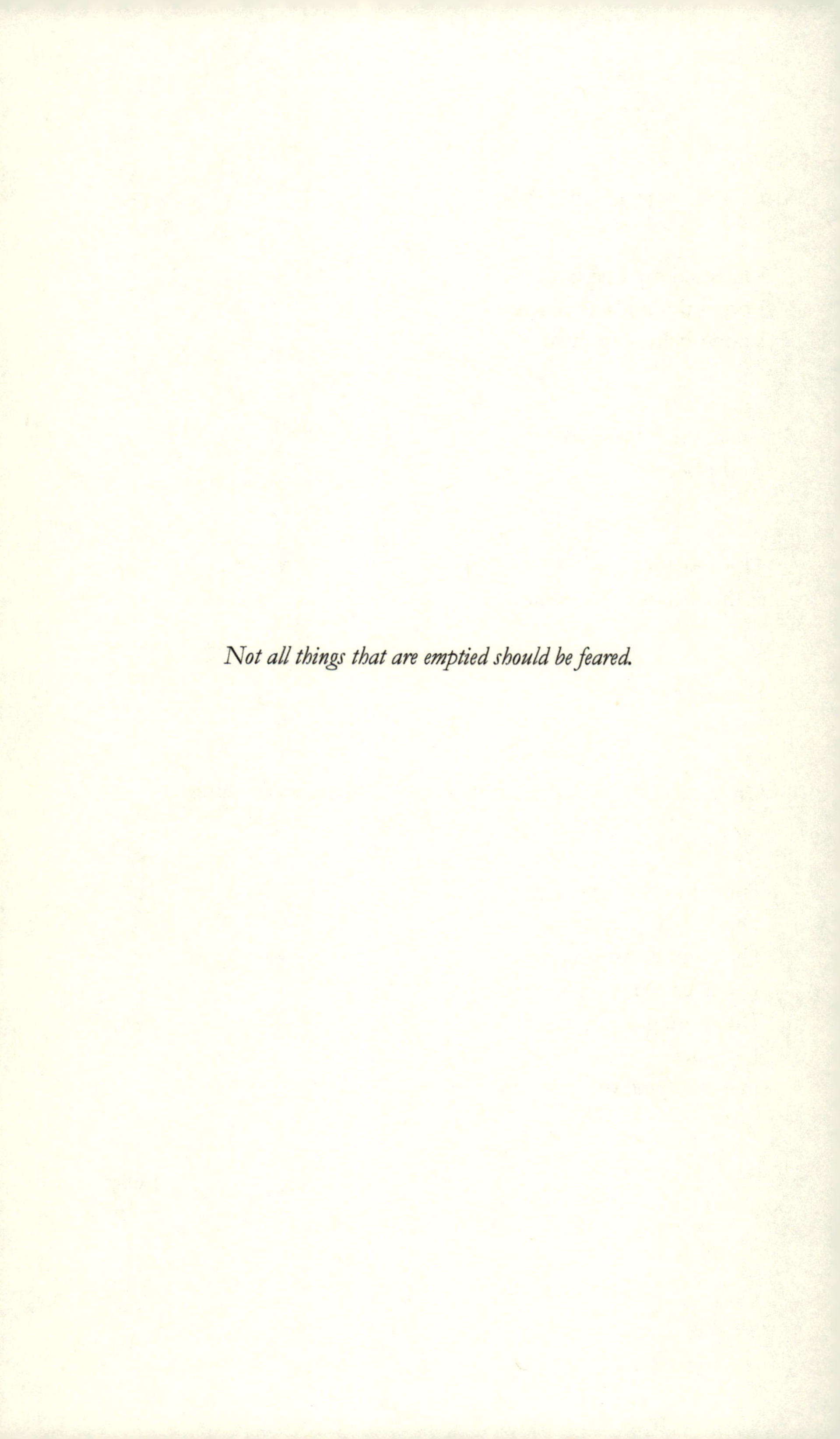

Not all things that are emptied should be feared.

CONTENTS

laden

F E E L

What if life is to feel it all?
To become a master of feeling.
Forgiving the unforgivable.
Loving with reckless abandon.

Being so angry
you break down and cry.

So sad
you begin to believe
the season will never change.

So joyful
your words turn into song.

So giving
your heart has no room
except to expand.

So still
you can feel the blood
moving through the body.

HARD

I didn't fit the mold.
Someone else did.

What could be
was never considered...
only what already was.

The only way to change
is to step out.
Not back in.

Step out,
desires mirrored.
Step in,
mirrored fears.

Choose your hard.

C L A S H

Two years since the great rattling.
One full life of living.
Or rather,
coping.

The flimsy foundation
finally collapsing.
Reaching to be pulled out
only pushed me further under.
Drowning.
Suffocating.

They will try to name it.
Crisis.
Phase.
A season that will pass.

I know the name.
Clash.
The life built out of necessity
against the life
never taken.

Flatlined grief.
A life that almost worked.
Now grasping for a nonexistent script.
Longing for neat rows of stability,

of my perfectly packaged,
quietly bracing,
carefully performed life.

Complaining about traffic
and racists
and religion
and safe arguments with predictable repercussions.

There's no returning to the box.

Authenticity.
A lonesome road.

Not happier...
Raw.
Every emotion ripping through the seams.
Bargaining to feel less.
Pleading to feel numb.

Living is harder
than hardly living.

Why does freedom feel like fear?
Why do walls give us a sense of safety?

What do we lose to stay small?

*I'm too far on all things
to turn back now.*

D U S T

When you are grieving,
seeing happiness in other people
becomes the most painful thing imaginable.

How dare they parade life moving forward
when mine feels like it has stopped in time.

The inner and outer worlds out of sync.

Grief doesn't hurry out the door.
It settles. It gathers. It moves in.
Sets up shop in private crevices.

What once was alive and thriving is now dust.

The more you try to clear it,
the more it returns,
floating in the air as a reminder
before resettling.

What if I just let it stay...
Let myself be a little dusty?

What if I let it be dusty for a while?

Stop fighting.

Accept the lived-in mess.

I'm tired of being sad
and sad of being tired.

I grieve a version of me
that was blissfully unaware.

Grieving who I was
before I knew what I now know.

I can't unknow.
But I feel unknown now.

She doesn't come back.
She has forever been changed.

At the end of my life,
will I say this was worth it?

The poet in me wants to believe yes...
wants romance, meaning, something alive.

The other part says it never was,
never will be.

Love... a lie in sheep's clothing.

I grieve something
that may have never existed
outside my own mind.

And maybe that's the worst grief of all...
the one you can't even believe was ever real.

No tidy ending.

Just dust.

split

D U A L

49 times 2.

Something I thought of as shame and failure now praised in headlines as success.

Independent woman. On my own.

I'm terrified.
Frozen.
Old tapes running
that I'm less than equal.

Failure stacked in my favor.
Future man to pick me up.

Mind clinging to marriage.
Body convulsing the arrangement.
Spirit breathing life after release.

And I still haven't stood up for myself.
I'm still small.

I'm a goddess
    I'm a wreck
I'm powerful
    I'm nothing on my own

I'm made for greatness
    I'm dumb and gullible
I'm overcoming barriers
    I'm clinging to agreements I never wanted
I love being a woman
    I hate being a woman
I am thriving
    I am dying
I am getting healthier
    I am deteriorating
I am creative
    I am in a slump
I know what is next
    I am so lost
I am so proud of how far I've come
    I am so ashamed of how long it is taking
I know my worth
    I apologize for leaving

Stuck between asking for equal
and compromising on minimal.

Wanting the open road.
Clinging to the city.

Scared of the life in my rearview mirror.
Scared of my own intuition.

Wondering why God abandoned me.
Wondering why I abandoned myself.

Crying out anyway.
While I stifle the scream.

The small me is begging
to stay in the light.
While I walked out
and curled into a ball.

My apartment has become a cave.
All that is left
protecting me from the elements.

When will I learn
that I am my own shelter.
Not a place.
Not a person.
But me.

I am the love story

I just don't believe it yet.

REED

A reed can only make sound
through emptiness.

All old fears and anxiety are driving.
Things that were clear
are now muddled.

I freeze.
I fawn.
I look for old guard rails.

I feel like that lost little girl
waiting for safety to appear.

Glancing back, it comes into focus...
I didn't fight for what I stood for.
I didn't fight for myself.

I kept people who weren't mine.
I kept jobs that weren't mine.
I kept things that weren't mine.

I've seen the world
but not the world I belong to.
The people.
The place.
The community.

I am a lone reed.

I miss that version of me,
The one so clear and confident.
She must be there somewhere.

When I lost the attachment
to all that was not me,
did I lose the attachment
to what really is me
as well?

D O O R

I defeated the dragon.
I was so focused on the fight,
I didn't notice
there was no map out.

The room has gone quiet.
The smoke is still settling.

I keep touching the walls,
looking for a door
that was never part of the plan.

Nobody tells you
this part.

How to leave

after you've won.

Waiting.
Waiting.
Waiting and pacing.
Waiting for answers

I fear will never come.

DREAM

Cities burning
as I watch from above.

My childhood home, empty.
Hardwood warm.
Soft cream walls.
Sheer curtains blowing
through open windows.

That's it.
That's the repeating dream.

A man I can't forget
but can no longer see.

I wander the city
waiting for something
to make sense.

The more I try,
the more it turns upside down.

Nothing to grip.
Even solid forms
are becoming
a mirage.

BOTH

Is this awakening
or dissociation?

Is it spiritual
or trauma?

I once said,

*I'm hearing from God
or I'm crazy.*

The response?

Why can't it be both?

I don't know a lot
but you don't know until you know,
but when you know,
you definitely know.

I do know a lot
about the things I know.

Just not much
about the things I don't know.

You know?

F O R C E

Crashing.
A wave breaking on the shore.
Vertigo.

Sometimes the body
will force
staying still.

All these ambitions
and now I see
it's from my ego.

Be bigger.
Be noticed.
Remembered.

All outward
so I don't go
inward.

Distractions are
no longer working.

What do I desire?
Inner stillness.

Simplicity.

Work where I see people
come alive.

To slow down.
To make something with my own hands.

A home surrounded
by art and comfort and love.

To travel by wandering
and being curious.

That's it — that's all.

The simplest is often
the hardest to achieve.

34

Towers crumble
We hold on to the familiar
And grieve what hasn't even fallen.

D E T O X

This couch...
Selected with just me in mind.
Jarring, honestly.
It's perfect...
Mine.

What is this that has come over me?

Doubt, sadness, fear,
perceived regret
all take over.

Sleepless nights.
Uncontrollable shaking.
Sweating through nightmares.
Congestion.
I lose my voice.

Shaming myself for how I respond.
I tell myself I've made the wrong decision.
Yet I know.

This is detox.

Something is leaving me
that has been bottled up
so long.

Withdrawal.

Addicted to a story
I've listened to far too long.

Addicted
to being small.

Addicted
to saying yes.

This couch...
the first thing
breaking my addiction.
It's perfect.

Mine.

W A L L

Dark walls.

Maybe it wasn't me drowning.
Maybe it was the version of me
that lived here
and I was willing
to let her die.

It was over.
Stillness melded into memory.

The dark wall stares back.
Tired of pretending
to hold everything up.

Instead of darkness bringing
cozy comfort,
the wound kept
bleeding.

Am I lost?

Or am I taking the long life
way around?

REFLIES

Selfies.

I'm thinking of calling them Reflies.

Reflections of me as I journey through
liminal time and space.
Little checkpoints.
A way to see how my light is doing.

This year?
Not good.

I woke up feeling like
I haven't tried hard enough
to keep my life together.
Turning back to myself,
I realized...

The one person I let down the most,
is me.

AGREEMENT

I wasn't good enough to be loved.

I lose love
if I don't keep my life together
the way everyone else wanted it to look.

I don't fit the mold.
I don't fit the system.
I am the problem.
I have to earn my place in the world.

Shattered.
Into irreparable pieces.

I believed the wrong storyline.

I had to let go of the full version of me,
built to be accepted.
The version
begging to be loved.

No longer able to hold the agreed story,
my world crumbles.

ABSORB

Vertigo.
Weight loss.
Anemia.
Hair falling out.
Surgeries.
Anxiety.
Depression.

Yet, the scariest part?
The light had gone behind my eyes.

I absorbed the blame.
The guilt.
The shame.
The fear.
All of it.

I apologized
for no longer being able
to hold that version of me up.

I owe myself the apology.

For allowing myself to get so far underwater
that when I finally reached out and said

I can't do this anymore,

the ones around me
allowed me to drown.

I've been paddling in the deep end for years.
I've been the flotation device for so long
that I forgot
my floatie needed a floatie.

Reflies showing no sign of life.
An empty vessel.
A shell of a human.

Walking past the mirror,
I'd see no one.
No Jaime.

Moments I thought I was already dead.

Like a gas stove
that wouldn't light.

CRAWL

Underwater.
No sense of up or down.
Helpless.
Terrified.
Lonely.
Debilitating.

My lively spirit dwindled.
My passion for exploring and movement
turning against me.

Darkness consumes fast.

Storyteller of life.
Processing instead of bottling.
Past me would repress and stay quiet.
Now learning to
Feel.
Breathe.
Share.

A few days ago I wandered out.
One smallest step at a time.
I stayed with my breath.
Wore my noise cancelling headphones.
Focused on small moments.
And I made it.

That evening I beat myself up
for not being stronger.
But as I lay in bed I shifted
and looked at what I did
that I couldn't even do
two days before.

You know the moments of deep despair?

The total collapse.
The anger.
The lamenting.

I gave up all control.

I give up!
Take this.
It's too much for me to carry.
I can't do this anymore.

That collapse was my surrender.

I've always prided myself on being strong.
Not needing anyone.
Always the helper.

But not this time.
I needed people.

And when I found myself alone
all I could do was cry out.

45

I'm not better.
But I see a glimmer.

I listened to my body
and told the world no
while I rested.

We find the bottom.
Cry out.
And slowly

learn to crawl.

Hope has been an anchor

drudged through the mud.
It felt too heavy.

But what if I had let go of hope?

S I G N A L

When God sends you to your destination
and it's not like the brochure.

I think I am a broken GPS.

Turn left.
But it's not paved.
No four-wheel drive.

I have a destination.
I plugged it in.
I took the route.
Detoured.
Stopped.
Hit potholes.
Construction.
Car breakdowns.
Surprise roadside attractions.
Mud.
Ditches.
Wrecked.
Coming out mangled and bruised.

I've even abandoned all
to walk the treacherous terrain
while shedding layers of protection.
You know the part —
take the rest of the way on foot.

I feel like I've arrived
armed with nothing.
Exposed completely to the elements.
Huddled in place
waiting for further guidance.

I scream at the sky —

Is this it, God?
This is not what you said would be here.

What if nothing comes after the clearing?
Worse yet —
what if only bad things come instead?

I'm waiting for 5G.
I have no service.
I hold my phone up to the sky.
Walk around.
Nothing.

Maybe I plugged it in wrong.
I've done that so many times.

All the doors are locked.
No way out.

Even when you lose your hearts,
your life —
you come back
to this same room.

Who is the biggest monster?
It's me.

I'm here
as I'm pelted by hail.

Earthquakes shake the towers
I built on no solid foundation.

Stripped of comforts.
Securities.
Precious promises.

Holding my dog
and what is left
of a carefully curated life.

Knowing the end of the story
shapes how you walk
through the middle.

HORIZON

I've survived.
Still unsure if I'm even alive.
Still unsure of what awaits me.

I have been faithful
to the call
down the worst road of my life.

35,000 feet
in full winged flight,
I see the horizon.

Screenshots predelete.
Mere screenshots
had turned into forward motion.

May I continue to not only believe
but obey.

May I remember the promises
when I have my feet

on the ground.

hollow

UNRAVEL

It didn't happen overnight.
It took years.

Shame, silence, judgment,
from others.
From myself.

The harder I tried,
the more I failed.
The more I failed,
the quieter I became.

Until I turned into someone
I didn't recognize.

And the church loved

that version of me.

PARADOX

The more I stepped away
the more free I became.
The more compassion I held.

The closer I felt
to walking the way
he would have walked.

Walking away
was the most spiritually
Christ-like decision
I've ever made.

ENOUGH

I set out to prove I was enough.
I walked in already convinced I wasn't.
For the Bible told me so.
Holy words…
fragmented by shame.

Looking for safety in belonging.
I left looking for the same.

Guilt, when it shows up,
has become a compass.
Not a punishment.
A signal.
A moment of realignment.

I am worthy.
I am shedding what never belonged to me.
I am no longer ruled
by the shame game.

HOME

This wasn't a falling away.
It was a falling inward.

The walk away was never a rejection.
It was an initiation.

A slow-burning, holy undoing
of everything that wasn't love.

I had to leave
in order to do
my most necessary healing work.

I had to leave
in order to find

Home.

EMBEDDED

I didn't show up consistently enough.
I failed many times over.
I can't even tell you when I broke.

But I did.

Chipped away.
A little bit in a college lobby.
Then again when a boy walked into my cabin bathroom
while I was showering at church camp.
I screamed and he didn't leave.

And again when a professor told his class
that I made men lust
when I did a tap routine on stage during chapel.

How would it look?
Nothing really happened.
They are such a good guy.
That would ruin their future.

Followed by laughter.
Dismissal.

Part of me still thinks all that is normal.
That I deserved that.
That I didn't protect men in power enough.

That is how embedded it becomes.
Embodied.

59

All under the church umbrella.
All under the blanket of love.

SPEAK

I've carried strollers up subway stairs
when someone's arms were shaking.

I've followed a man
to the end of the subway line
to feed a cat.

I've let a stranger's child
fall asleep on my shoulder
on the train.

I've walked unhoused
in zero-degree temps
to nearby shelters.

I've sat in safe houses
with mothers and their children
who fled domestic violence.

I've cried with a 14-year-old grieving girl
who had an abortion
after being raped by her father,
worried she was going to hell.

A young man collapsed into my arms
during a pride parade.

He started crying
and all I could say was —

      I'm so sorry.
      I'm so very sorry.

Not once did we speak about Jesus.

But goodness,

                         did he speak.

Eleventh grade.
Severe pain.
Crying.
Begging to die
or make it stop.

The room filled with presence.

F O G

I sang it tonight
with a candle in my hand,
the same way I did
in this very church
when I was thirteen years old.

Same song.
Same warm glow.
Same tradition.

Afterwards,
fog consumed the air
down dark country roads.
The same roads
since I was eighteen.
The same Christmas music
for decades.

But familiar roads
and familiar songs
do not mean
everything is familiar.

Being in darkness is one thing.
Being in the dark with fog
is another entirely.

In the dark,
light can still reach you

In the fog,
all light struggles
to find its way.

I was clinging to the steering wheel,
praying I was on the right path,
praying I was being protected.

God rarely sends me
down rational paths.

There is uncertainty.
Fear.
Displacement.
Danger.
No clear plan.
No sense of safety.

When I was sixteen
I went to tell my great grandmother
about a decision I had made.
I was euphoric.
Convinced this would make life easier.

She listened.

Then said,

> *Remember this feeling.*
> *Your life will never be*
> *as easy as it is today.*
> *Your true journey starts now.*
> *God will challenge you*
> *and you won't want to listen.*

I thought she was wrong.
I was the exception.

She was right.

So I enter the fog
with a candle in my hand.

One day the fog will lift.

And this little light of mine
will come shining through

                    the dark.

THORN

Pain demands attention.
Shouts from the rooftops.
Screams loud enough
to cast aside faith,
willpower,
logic.

Anger fills the space.

I keep thinking of the thorn.
Prayed for it to be taken away.
Praised through weakness.

Sometimes what was meant to heal
begins to hurt.

I will praise you

                    in this thorn.

WEAK

I'm clinging.
I'm not strong.
But I don't have to be.

The stories that flood the space:

I'm weak.
I deserve this pain.
I'm not brave enough.
I'm not strong enough.

Maybe surgery was a mistake.
Maybe I could have endured without.

God's strength is
showing
in my weakness.

I'm not strong.

But I don't have to be.

The Bible doesn't begin with order.
It begins with chaos.
Separating light from darkness.
Life from chaos.

DOUBT

How quickly
beliefs dissolve.

It scares me.
Not what I might do,
but how fast
Hope
disappears.

I am most excellent
at arguing,
bargaining,
doubting,
shouting.

Pro level.

I spend most of my life
in uncertainty.
More questions than answers.

But still showing up
in the middle
of a very important conversation.

My doubts?
My tantrums?
My questioning?

They don't disqualify me from faith.

It's a humble faith.
A raw faith.

I'm still here.

Even among the doubt.

H E A L

A tiny act of trust
in a breath.
A gentle hand on my heart.

A whispered —

this is temporary.

Belief dissolves.
Truth arrives.

I choose the work of light.

exposed

FAULT

I take the pup outside
as she begrudgingly pees,
pulling me back to the door.

She is so irritated
that I woke her up for this.

OK old friend,
your voice is heard.

On my own,
I meander and find a bench,
welcoming the break in the fresh air.

A little girl shrieks in the distance
and I feel the rise in my body.
Is it fear for her
or my own internal screams?

Morning dove.
Kids cheering.
The silent awakening of the city that never sleeps.

Fresh fertilizer.
Dogs strollin'.
The collide of death and rebirth.
The hope of darkness lifting.

The silly early optimists
rising from the ground.

Stagnant water.
Forgotten trash.
My long shadow.

Trains rattling in the distance,
brakes squeezing as they pull into the station.

The brisk early light hitting my face.

Man wearing a suit and a baseball cap.
The dichotomy of life
shoved into clothing.

I sit still on a bench
with 30 years of layered paint,
the paint chipped enough to see the layers,
the natural wood bleeding beneath.

A fallen leaf blows through the breeze along the ground,
bumping into new growth.

He believes his life is over,
dormant and lost in the cold,
as he stares back at the trees

that abandoned him above.

Does he not realize he is free?

If you sit here long enough,
the ebb and flow begins to show itself.

The only way to catch this
is to stay still and notice.

Otherwise,
you
are part of the ebb and flow.

Self reflection can be painful.

I wonder how many people
hear their own voice in their head.

Maybe that is why people talk out loud.
Otherwise they would feel crazy.

What if my chosen words create the wrong emotion.
Now we have found a rooted fear.

Not all things planted are beneficial.
Once it allowed safety,

but it has gotten out of hand.

For a moment,
I have stepped out of that world
and into noticing
thanks to this bench.

>   *Hey, you.*
>   *Look around.*
>   *You are safe.*

I rise and carry on my walk.

I really did just plan
for a boring walk.

The rest was the bench's fault.

I disappear on foot.
I disappear into rhythm.
I disappear into causes.
I disappear into people
and sidewalks
and clackity tracks
and crumbling concrete
and hustle
and graffiti
and forgotten stones.

S T I L L

Pipes clank
signaling warmth is to come.

A dog barks.
Yips dampened
by the blanket of white fluff.

He gets closer,
amplified
between the heavy hundred-year-old brick.

The snow has gotten into his soul.

Neighbor above me
loves to wear shoes in his apartment.
Why hasn't he learned
to walk lightly?

Kids begin to filter out
to the mini hill
and leave tracks
in the freshly fallen untouched snow.

A moment that can't be put back
this round.
We have to wait
for the next snow fall.

Hybrid car whistles
as they turn around
on my dead end street.
One way in.
A maze to get out.

I lay cuddled in my bed
missing my dog.

Thinking of the tourists
currently walking Central Park —
not realizing
even eight years in,
you don't get to see it like this.

But I know it's out there.
Waiting for me to claim it
if I choose.

And for today
that is enough.

I choose the moment I am in
out of the moments

I'm allowed to choose.

Like the city in snow —
it's when I realize
how loud it has been.

BRACE

I had become so hard here.
Not in the way you'd think.
Hard as in bracing.

Bracing for the next noise,
next shatter,
next impact.

You know how drunk drivers
walk away unscathed?
They are loose.
They bend.

That's how this city has become for me.
That's how life is becoming.

Not overnight.
Not one big aha.

But with a walk when I broke.
With a pause with a mother.
With a smile at a young child.
With a gift of a muffin to the hungry.
With a click of a volunteer submission form.
With a letting go of a secure job.
With a letting go of a secure marriage.
With a letting go of controlling my health.

With a letting go of financial latching.

Letting go of material items.
Letting go of the need for others to see my good works.
Letting go of needing life to have meaning.
Permission to move forward
with my own spiritual knowing.

It's gotten easier to discern.
But oh so lonely.

Things don't have to make sense
to anyone else.
Not even me.

I follow.
I obey.

And honestly —
now that I'm on this track
I'm really curious

what he is up to.

CURVES

The way I feel the curves of the subway
is the same way I felt the backroads
to my grandparents' farm.

I still feel the up and down
of the two hills
I know I should have gone slower over.

I feel it the same way I know
the gentle curve in the country road
from St. Louis to Jacksonville.

I could tell you the exact moment
a stop sign will show up
entering the small town
with the 25 speed limit.

I could tell you which intersection
a cop would be sitting
behind a cornfield.

This is the muscle memory of life.

We pay attention with our eyes
but also with the cadence
and rhythm
of what we know.

I close my eyes on the subway
reach my stop
blink open
and I'm there.

We learn as we go.
We become part of the symphony
around us.

DEGREE

Warm December weather takes me out
before the winds and cold creep in.

I walk toward the path,
but an internal pull
takes me into the woods instead.

The curiosity of a child
enters my body
as I climb through old cobwebs
and stomp through brush
and crunchy leaves.

My muscles begin to fire.
Childhood muscles
that have gone missing
from flat safe pavements.

Small fears enter.

    What if I fall and hit my head?
    What if no one finds me?

Then bigger competing fears
keep me moving forward.

*What if my body forgets
what being a child is like?
What if I spend my whole life
being scared?
What if I look back with regret
over the things I didn't do
out of fear?*

Yes.
Those are much worse fears.

I am the girl who follows adventure.
The girl who tested velocity off bridges,
climbed trees,
played in the dirt
under a canopy of leaves.
The girl who went down the slide normal once
and hung upside down on monkey bars.
The girl that wondered what that button does
and touched wet paint.

The path I'm on
wasn't created for me.
I am having to find it
on my own.

When you are walking inside your fear,
you become aware of everything.

The ground.
The branches.
The sounds.
The silence.

Things find me
instead of being placed for me to find.

I make it.
The bottom of the hill.
Feet away from the creek.

Beautiful.
Quiet.
My heart beating.
My nervous system alive.

Then the question comes...

How do I get back up?

Back on the paved trail
where I belong.
(so they say)

Still beautiful.
But less of my body is involved.
Less of my mind.

My story becomes the same as everyone else's.
Linear.
Not mine.

How quickly the path
wants us to forget
what can be found
if we deviate
just a degree.

Maybe the path keeps us safe
or maybe the path keeps us asleep.

A teenager with hot pink hair
coasts along on an electric bike,
arms out wide toward the trees.
Head tipped upward.
Soaking in the warm sunlight
reaching her through the clouded skies.

She welcomes the breeze
and lets the path carry her
without effort.

Her own path
while on the path.

Off the path is a secret path.
A degree or two away.

*I don't want to live
someone else's story anymore.*

T O L L

Fourteen years ago
I stood still long enough
to hear church bells
echo through centuries-old buildings,
bouncing off cobblestone streets
acting like they had somewhere important to be
and at the same time
were in no rush to get there.

I daydreamed...
how amazing would it be
to live in a city
and hear bells every day.

I've lived in this apartment four years.
They never rang.
Not once.

And then this year
they started.

Every day.
12:15pm.
6pm.

Just waiting for me to need them.

I asked my favorite neighbor,
half expecting her to tell me
I was imagining things.

She lit up immediately.

Oh my God, I've heard them too.
Isn't it amazing?
I love them.

We didn't solve anything.
But there was comfort
in knowing I wasn't alone
in noticing.

Awe and wonder isn't rare.
It's just often unspoken,
hidden in our grown-up get-ups.

I was practicing my cursive.
The slow, somatic rhythm
of pen on paper.
The loops.
The pressure.
The little inconsistencies
that prove I am human.

My hand is not as steady.
Not as sure.

Handwriting... like bells... like noticing...
becoming an art
we don't quite hold onto anymore.

It brings me back to my grandparents:
their notes, their recipes,
their jokes scribbled on notepads
and scraps of paper.

Little pieces of them
carried forward through ink.

Last night I was moving so fast
I sliced my finger open.
The kind of cut
that makes you stop
whether you want to or not.

All of it
because I was hurrying through a life
that wasn't asking me to.

Nothing around me
required me to hurry.

It was just me.

So here I am.

Bandaged finger.
Pen in hand.

Finally sitting still long enough
for the bells I once dreamed about

                                        to toll.

95

*I just needed to stop long enough
to let them find me.*

SNOWDROP

If you live long enough,
you begin to notice the rhythms.
The small ones first.
The places where things return.

I knew they'd be waiting for me.
I knew the street.
I knew the angle of the sun.
I knew the snowdrops would have returned.

When lacrosse sticks come out on the field again.
When the heaviness in the air begins to lift.
When the doves return to their perch on the fire escape.

When the mockingbird sings again,
mimicking car alarms and sirens
until even the city noise
becomes part of the enchanting melody.

When the coughing lady tosses peanuts out her window
for the squirrels.

These small returns begin to stack up.
Quiet confirmations
that the world still remembers
how to move forward.

And yet.

This year I feel an undercurrent running below.
Closed eyes. Little asks.

That this won't be the spring the darkness refuses to lift.
That this won't be the spring conflict tears through our streets.
That this won't be the spring without a free nation.
That this won't be the last spring
I walk these same paths through the city.

You live long enough
and you begin to pray
small seasonal prayers.

And still...
The snowdrops come.
Small white bells
bending toward the ground.

Chloe stands among them,
nose low to the earth,
as if she's known this rhythm
all along.

And we pause
for a moment

in the middle.

L O V E D

I was in Central Park,
in the Ramble,
when I learned
the Pet Memorial Tree
had been cut down.

For years,
people left photo Christmas ornaments,
little tokens of pets
they had loved and lost.

A living shrine.
Forty years.

But the very weight of that love
weakened it.
The branches overloaded.
And finally gave in.

It had been loved to death.

Standing in the Ramble
with all the world's woes,
I broke too.

The tree became my doorway.

I found the release
my body decided
it could handle.

Our nervous system is a container.
It can only hold so much
before it spills over.

The body looks for a smaller doorway
to let the feeling out.

A forgotten memory.
A song.
A tree cut down.

The body whispers —

 here,
 cry here —

and lets us reset
just enough
to keep moving.

I wanted to walk up the steps
of my old apartment
when my dreams were still young
before the world felt like it was crumbling.

L O U I S

The place I had to put my dog down
and walk back alone
at 1am
numb to the pain.

The place of my breaking point,
crying in the street
and yelling.

The place I let go
of the world's expectations.

The place that held my dreams.

Even in the moments
of such sadness and fear.

A joke and a smile
from the laundromat owner.
A check-in from my fruit guy.
Flowers blooming through the sidewalk.
Piano playing in a small apartment.

Small moments
reminding me
I was on my path.
The place that finally released me

to give me somewhere
to call my own.

Allowing another life

                              to bloom.

M U F F L E D

Snow dampens the city
stripping away illusion
comforting the deafening sounds.

Silence pours into my apartment.

Muscles fight against the shift of the city.
Where has everyone gone?

Hope lost.
Breath. My only companion.

The smell of browning butter. Cookies.

The little girl in me wanders into the hallway.

Could it be, I'm not alone?

The downward journey begins.
Basement level.

The eerie echo of the elevator's mechanical woman announces the
floor.
I wish she'd say more.

Laundry room. Sterile, clean.
No fighting for machines.
No hovering over timers.
No passive-aggressive shuffling of someone else's clothes.

All to myself.

What a dichotomy.
What a conundrum.

What a hypocrite.

To miss the mild irritation.
The side-eyes.
The quiet competition for a dryer.

Because here... that's the beginning.

The New York way.

We pretend to be bothered.
We test each other first.
A glance.
A pause.
A moment of... are you safe? Are you real?

And then...

Dogs.
Weather.
Where'd you get that coat.

Warmth. Disguised as annoyance.

The warmth of my clothes brings me back to myself.
Simple.

I begin to settle into the silence
and the warmth
so opposite to my winter city days.

Alone.
But not alone.

I wonder about neighbors a little too often.
I wonder if they wonder about me.

When we all don't see each other,
does anyone else worry?

Such a strange fear that settles in
when you're alone in the city.

Morbid? Yes.
But it lingers.

Will anyone find me
if I went missing?

How long
before someone asks questions?

When the city goes quiet

                        the mind goes loud.

INTACT

I walk in
and instantly know —
this smells like New York City
when I was sixteen.

I look up.
I was right.

Think of all the smells in the world.
Thirty three years later
and I named it
without sight.

After everything.
The senses still work.
Something survived.

If I can trust this
can I trust

the rest?

bare

HIDDEN

This isn't a story about him.

This is a story about how I made myself
small
and hidden
to stay safe.

I asked to be removed
from directory information.
I stopped performing.
I requested my name
not show on websites.

I changed my name
and hoped
he couldn't find me.

Once a month
I googled myself
to make sure
nothing would pop up.

But something else happened.

I began to change.
I adapted.
I closed myself off

to opportunities.

I did not want
to be seen
or found.

I wonder how much of this
has spilled.
I fear.
I know.

How many people.
How many opportunities.

Pushed away
to keep myself

safe.

The city's loud.
I'm louder.

I breathe with the sirens
and still find grace.

O W E

I have panic attacks of being seen.

Coming from the girl
who loved being on stage.
Who loved helping people.
Being of service
to whatever was needed.

She buried herself.
And all the good
that came with her.

I owe her so much.

I want her to be proud.
I want her to know
what we have been through
is worth it.

This fire in me
asks for air.

What must burn
will burn.
From the ashes,
new growth arrives.

FIERCE

All my theories in life
seem to be about power.
Not about obtaining power.
About rising above oppression.
About suppressing
those who suppress.

Midlife
and feel like I'm coming
into my own.

I am wise.
I think I am beautiful.
I have finally discovered
I am not stupid
like I was told.

So why do I feel
more alone
and erased
than ever before?

S L Y

We bought into a lie
that as women
we are only good
when we are young.

Oh you mean —
we could only be controlled
when we were young.

How terrifying
that as we age
we become more fierce.

I've been told I'm intimidating.

Me.
Polite.
Kind.
Compassionate.

But yes
after a long hiatus
tail between my legs
I have a voice again.

Intimidating?

Hell no.

Powerful?

                              Damn straight.

The church?

                              Submission.

The workplace?

                              Professionalism.

Marriage?

                              Compromise.

Influencers telling women
how to look
and what to buy?

                              Perfection.

Oppression continues
in a sly little dance.

*There is a hot zone
right on the perimeter.
Take it to the edge
and watch it expand.*

EMBER

Gone are the days
of power suits
and shoulder pads.

Flowy dress with leather jacket…
holding my feminine
and masculine sides.
Softness with edge.

Our strength is harnessed from within.
We've been taught to smother.

But the embers
are still at a slow burn.

We know that's where
mesmerizing restraint
and fiercest heat
live together.

My prose interrupted…
a man encouraging his wife.
A gentle kiss.

You've got this.
Harness all your internal power.
No one does you better than you.

He sees her.

Our bodies are beautiful
because essence glows there.

We turned to flames
and they tried to smother.

But now we are ember.

Let's stay ember,
and watch what catches light.

OXYGEN

Hits off my light are not free.
They come at a cost.

Like a drug,
you'll want more.

Stay in the dark
or come into the light.

Don't lurk in my wilderness
while you escape to your dungeon
guarded by dragons.

I've knocked at closed doors
for too long.

I don't belong in the dungeon
anyway.

I'm walking around
with heart wide open.
Only a shield between us.

New breath is entering
through the gaping wounds.

It's starting to hurt
less and less.

121

Blood loves oxygen.

                                        And so does fire.

BRUISED

I have such a fear
of history repeating itself.

Once hurt or disappointed,
I go into full shutdown.
I change direction
and never look back.

Well.
Almost never.

I faced my fear of returning to dance.

Afraid I was too old,
too out of shape,
not talented enough,
not confident enough.
Not good enough.

When I finally dove back in,
I fell hard and fast.

My body could still recall
a shuffle step,
a pull back,
arabesque,
plié.

Something in me recognized
what had been missing
and I came back alive.

March 14, 2020.

My last class.

The next day,
the world changed.

I had finally faced my fears
and was welcomed with a clobbering.

Part of me shames her for her naïveté.

Another part wants to take her by the shoulders —

>   *Of course you believed.*
>   *Of course you did.*
>   *That's what hope looks like*
>   *before it's been bruised.*

During the pandemic
I took my tap shoes with me.
I practiced in every garage I could find.
I hadn't given up.

How many times do you think
I've been back to dance
since I returned to the city?

Once.

My body wouldn't cooperate.
It failed to remember
what had once come naturally.

I felt old.
Out of shape.
Not talented.
Not confident.

The things I had feared years prior
finally showed up.
Delayed.

So I quit.

I told myself it didn't matter.
I told myself my time had passed.
I had failed.

But wouldn't you know
something sprouted anyway.

A small seedling.

I don't scream at things to grow anymore.
I don't drown them with effort
or poison them with expectation.

I tend to them softly.
I notice them.
I protect them.
I protect me.

I don't fully trust it.
I'll show up knowing
it could disappear.

Small steps.
Small movements.
A ball change, maybe.
Maybe?

Forget talent.
Forget confidence.
Forget fear.

I'm going back
to let my body speak
in whatever broken, beautiful sentences
it still knows.
Heart open.

Yet guarded.

Choosing to dance anyway.

This isn't naïveté.

*It's unrequited hope —
still choosing to move
in the only way I know how.*

GRIP

I still have it on cassette.
I carry it sometimes in my hands
and grip it close to my heart
as if it holds
all my innocent childhood memories.

If I keep it close,
I can keep that version of me close too.

I'm not sure why I worry
I'll lose her
if I loosen the grip.

Warm inside.
Cold outside.

I'd sit in the back seat
and watch my warm breath condense,
competing with the frost
forming on the windows.

The tape deck had an auto flip.
Even now, when I stream,
I still hear the imaginary click
after the appropriate song.

I would sit in front of the tree for hours.

Watching the twinkles.
The bubble lights.

I'd count,
waiting for the moment
they started to bubble.
One by one.

I'd try to guess
which one would be brave enough
to bubble first.
Then which one would follow.

A small game with no consequence
between me and the tree.

I play it on vinyl now.
But it's my portal back
to the cassette version.

Such power

                                        in something so simple.

UNTOUCHED

Easter morning.
Windows down.
Country music playing.
Because that's just what you do
when you're back in the Midwest.

I stopped in my hometown
to visit the gravesites.

Grandparents.
Great-grandparents.

Flowers left.

I had prepared my heart for that visit.

I was not prepared
for what came next.

The theater boarded up.
The gazebos forgotten.

The barrenness brought everything back
in flashes.

Memories that live in the senses

more than the mind.

The past shot back
into my present.

These grounds saved me.

Theater saved me.

I met my best friend here
when I was sixteen.
Rediscovered myself here.
Healed from heartbreak here.
Began to believe in myself again here.

Across from the theater,
the gazebos.

I remember admiring the people
who performed there
like they were stars.

I wonder if they ever knew
how amazing I thought they were.

Has anyone ever looked at me
the way I looked at them?

This was a chapter of life
that felt simpler.
When only my problems seemed big
and the world's felt small.

A little naive maybe.
But kind of beautiful too —
that I got to live in a moment
where I could be
that self-centered.

By the time I was back on the road
I realized I hadn't prepared my heart
properly after all.

The real grief hit me then.

Not at the cemetery.

But in realizing
I'm no longer naive
to the suffering of the world.

It's a different kind of loss.

The grief of no longer being untouched.
No longer thinking only of myself.

There is something to be said for being unfinished.

Where we can blame the missing piece for not being enough.

So much fear in feeling complete.

CANYON

I am integrating.

The parts of me
I had kept hidden
in my adult life to protect me —
I'm not putting them away anymore.

Working on my puzzle
with the missing piece.
It feels foreign.

My bold and safe ways don't work anymore.
My softness calls out.
Asks me to embrace and let the mask go.

Skin so fresh and bare.
Nowhere for scars to hide.

Fragile and wild.

I don't know how to be this person in my world.

The world of structure
and expectation
and pleasing the peoples.

My usefulness has made me feel used.

I hold a vision.
The canyon is made of vastness and depth.
I see the other side.

Do I crawl?
Do I trace the edge?
Do I go the long way around?

Or do I glide over on the promise

of faith?

TEND

I feel the guilt.

The walls feel like they are falling in on me.
Stuck in freeze state.
Not sure how to escape.

But it's not the guilt of wanting out.

It's the guilt of leading a half led life
and closing off a truth
I never wanted to admit.

That's what I feel the most guilty about.

That I dragged other people and myself
through a world
I was only trying to survive.

Survive what, you ask.

The carefully curated life.
The one that protects me from truly feeling,
truly risking,
one truly and undeniably mine.

There is a picture of me in my mind.

An aura. A calling. Me. Yet fully lit.

A light shoots through me
down into the earth
and up into the sky.
It vibrates when I start to stray.

I see things so clearly now
in my soul mirror.

Being asked to let everything
that doesn't align
fall away.

A clearing of all the channels
so whatever is meant for me
becomes magnetic.

I've been promised nothing.

I will be unveiled.

I see the vision.
Nothing specific.
But welcoming and warm and bright.

This guilt is not a threat.
It's a guide.

To awaken.

Yes, I've been spooked into freeze
like I saw a ghost.
Because awakening is scary as hell.

When you make plans and dream and hope
yet you chose an altered life...
of course guilt will follow.

I know what this costs.
I see it. I feel it.

Yet I've seen a light I can't unsee.

Wouldn't you tell me to run towards that light?

It's what I would tell anyone else to do.

At some point,
that little light of yours
will be up to you to protect.

I tend to that light.

And to the little girl
who is struggling to carry it...

I ask her on occasion
what she wants.
What she needs.

A whisper echoes in my body
a reluctant plea
I need you.
It's all I ever needed.

Please

Love me.

ROCK

Not as brave today.

There is a young girl in me
who comes out to ask
if we are still ok.

So I rock her.
And myself.

As I try to believe
what I tell her:

> *We are safe.*
> *We are warriors*
> *who do not need wars.*

YES

If I would have known the pain
I would not have said yes.
This is why when God asks,

are you ready?

he doesn't tell you what it will require.
Just your answer.

Right now I'm in hell.
No guarantee
that anything will be different.
Or even better.
Maybe worse.

But somewhere among all the doubt
there is a flicker.
A spark.

And the minute you find that —

                    the yes inevitably follows.

scoured

ENDURE

I remember the time
when signs and fate
were cute.

I'm over it.

None of them believe their way
into transformation.

They endure their way into it.

I don't believe in romance anymore.
Not because it failed me.
But because belief
turned out to be
unnecessary.

The things that were true
didn't need me
to hold them up.

Maybe belief isn't the highest form of faith.

Maybe non-belief
is what finally lets God move
without my interference.

One day, I felt clear.
The next, back in the fog.

What remains
when belief
is no longer
doing the work?

REMAINS

Let the night be blank.
Let God be quiet without being absent.
Let yourself not know
without self-abandoning.

Sometimes the thing holding you back
is the thing you are trying to hold on to.

Let it fall away.

                                        What remains
                                        was always yours.

FOREST

Love songs.
Rom coms.
Poems.

I go through stages
where I love them
and other times
want nothing to do with them.

The mere thought
and I shut down.
Walk away.

It's not the things that change.
It's my experience outside of them
that skews my view
of the very things
I claimed to love
and believe in.

I want to run.
Push it away.
Tell myself it's not real.

I get jealous of others
who still believe.

And most of all
I'm jealous
that it was taken from me.

That innocence.
That hope.

The sadness of being jaded.

Did I outgrow them?
Are they the fools?

But I go back.

And I begin to see
even in rom coms,
love songs,
poems...
there is always
a dark forest.

Maybe it wasn't shown.
Maybe it happens
after the credits roll.

And slowly

                              I begin to believe again.

Maybe if the dream is dead long enough,
the ghosts will subside as well.

SHADOW

We have walked in the dark so long
that we have made it to safety.

As the light appears
so do our deepest shadows.

What a terrible thing to see.

How we beg to be plunged
back into the darkness.

But we can't unsee.

We watch as the light rises
and shadows fade.

We see beauty in the shadows.
We notice everything
the light is touching.

When the dark comes back
we remember what was shown
and the light
will always arrive.

Shadows were never anything to fear.

We can't blame the light
for us finally being able to see
what we had tried
to keep hidden.

This was never about
looking at the shadow.
It's about what creates them.

Going back into the darkness
does not erase fear.

Sitting in the light
does.

152

Not all shadows are dangerous.

F L O A T

I was watching the leaves
change colors
and fall.

What if we tried to stop it?

We would waste our energy
and consume precious time
on a task
that would still lead
to the inevitable.

What if we judged this change?

What if we told the leaves
they weren't allowed
that green is the only way
to be a leaf?

What if we told the leaf
that the only way to contribute
was to hang on to the branch?

Sometimes we have to allow ourselves
to change.

Sometimes we have to allow ourselves
to fall.

Let the wind take us
where we might.

There are times to hold on.

But when the seasons change
in our own life
sometimes letting go,
letting our old selves die,
and planning for the rebirth
is the only option.

There is beauty in the free fall.

We think we will crash.

But it can feel like floating.

ROUND

Growth is expansive.
Never ending.

It asks us to let things fall away
while drawing closer at the same time.

Not linear.
Infuriating.

Exhausting.
Exhilarating.
Painful.
Mournful.

Right when we think we have it figured out?

Another round.

God?
Is this the point?
Is this what you want of me?
Is this the calling that I have answered?

WINGS

Fear of being alone at the top.
Fear of leading others
the wrong direction.
Fear of being so certain
and then uncertain.

It's not fear of failure
if you are a people pleaser.
It's fear of letting people down
with your success.

Sometimes the people
who support you now
will be the ones
who try to tear you down the most
as you climb.

Your goal is not to fit in
to the societal norms.
It's to create your own way.

Maybe it's not about foundation.
But about learning
how to use your wings.

Finding the branches
sturdy enough

to bend and hold you
at the same time.

You were never meant

                              to be on solid ground.

The dreamers, the artists, the free spirits
flowing between a society of
leaders and followers.

R E A S O N

He asked her why she loved him.

And she couldn't answer.

I asked him,
do you know why she should?

Are you looking for the reason
yourself?

BELL

Try
Fall
Try
Fall
Try
Fall

Stand two minutes
Collapse again.

Rise
Fall
Rise longer
Fall softer
Rise again

Stop swinging
and let the bell ring.

Because no healing happens in the ring
Healing happens in the corner.

Right now, my body pleads...

> *Please stop trying to be okay.*
> *Please stop trying to interpret this.*
> *Please just let me rest.*

I'm not getting up.

I'm staying here.
I'm not going to fix it.

                                        I'm letting the bell ring.

LIGHT

I am safe.
I am held.
I am steady.
I am breathing.
I am supported.
I am present.
I am protected.
I am grounded.
I am whole.
I am love.
I am capable.
I am strong.
I am complete.
I am provided.
I am trusting.
I am peace.
I am growing.
I am light.

LAND

My soul is homeless right now.

Long unhurried conversations.
Shared meaning.
Emotional honesty.
Bearing witness to someone's inner world.
Letting someone bear witness to yours.

Feeling chosen.
Not just tolerated.

In the Midwest, I'm too much.
In NYC circles, I'm too tender.

I'm in the wrong season
of the right journey.

The Midwest feels suffocating.
NYC feels too much.
Anywhere new feels impossible.

Can I land anywhere yet?

*Better discomfort in truth
than comfort in misalignment.*

released

VOICE

I'm having to get so small
so quiet
so still
to find it
to hear it.

Maybe it's little Jaime
I hid all those years ago.

Maybe it's my soul intuition.
Maybe it's the Holy Spirit.

Maybe I'm just a crazy person
who has lost their mind
on this crazy spinning rock.

Maybe it's all of the above.

R E A L

I live in New York City.

Real.

I'm getting divorced.

Real.

I have failed in my marriage.

Not real.

We are watching the fall of democracy.

Real.

I believe it is all unfolding
as intended.

Real.

I am my most beloved.

Real.

I forgot to fill my cup first.

Real.

I am learning.

Real.

M A R B L E

The city is the perfect place
for broken people.

It tells you
who do you need me to be?

Some come to reinvent.
Some come to escape.
Some come to unveil
to be chiseled
out of marble.

New York City
is the best disorder.

No apology
for its million personalities.

I'm not a city girl.
I'm not a country girl.
I'm just a girl.

Walking in wonder
as I wander in waiting.

Is my silence louder than my screams?

EXORCISM

I am in a season
where I hope meaning will return
after safety.

Tonight I went for a short drive.

Instinctively,
I screamed.

I didn't even recognize me.

The sound that emerged —
I'm not sure it came from my throat.

My heart?
My back?
My soul?

My soul.

Yes.

After the scream, I yelled.

There.

That's more like it.

I yelled and cursed and said things
I worried would seep out of the car windows
and be carried in the air
and land on the wrong recipient.

Just me and God
in the dark.

Oh, you better believe
God heard that first scream.

No judgment.
No condemnation.
No anger or scolding.

Just the feeling
of not being alone.

Quiet.
But not at all absent.

Before, he felt absent.
Now he fills the quiet.

For months I've been holding it together.
My throat tight

from holding my tongue
and my hurt
and my fear.

In a millisecond of safety,
the scream came to the surface.

                              The car filled with presence.

I see me.

And now
I'm closing the gap.

RAINBOW

I knew early on
I was born into a broken world.
But the song gave me hope.

I thought if everyone
could just listen

things would change.

My little optimistic spirit
would collapse
watching adults
slowly go back
to their daily lives.

Nothing healed.

I came in from the cold rain.
Through the window

a rainbow.

                              Someday we'll find it.

S T A R

I look up nightly.
Knowing they are there,
just beyond sight.

I am so small.
So inconsequential.
Yet, I was awakened for this.

The one light broke through.

Faith and longing colliding
in an east facing window.

Both of us learning to be the steady light.

I do not believe in coincidences.

Someday we'll find it.

RETURN

Today is February 27, 2026.

I look ahead
and still have no clue
where I'm going.
Part of me used to love that.

This raw, naked, vulnerable version of me
is terrified.

But I'm proud.

Whatever that voice was,
I listened.
I followed.

Someday I will say I'm grateful.
It's just not today.

And for the first time in a year,
I'm taking steps forward.

Baby steps.

More water.
More nature.

Long periods of rest.
Snuggling my dog.
Working on gentleness.
Making life easier.
Not harder.

And taking Reflies along the way

                        to check out the returning light.

The tower and destruction are complete.
The ground is being prepped.

Whatever comes next,
let it be loving and kind and true.
Without begging.
Without compromising.
Without minimizing or shrinking myself.

May I not dim myself again.

LEANING

Love,
Love,
Love,

Falling into love.

Heartbreak.

Falling into hate.
Falling into anger.
Falling into blame.
Falling into jealousy.
Falling into resentment.
Falling into avoidance.
Falling into distraction.
Falling into comparison.
Falling into perfectionism.
Falling into despair.
Falling into darkness.
Falling into nothing...

Nothing,
Nothing,
Nothing, still.

Still,
Still,

Stillness.

Leaning into grief.
Leaning into light.
Leaning into awakening.
Leaning into prayer.
Leaning into forgiveness.
Leaning into thankfulness.
Leaning into joyfulness.
Leaning into rejoicing.
Leaning into celebration.
Leaning into acceptance.
Leaning into peace.
Leaning into life.

Leaning into love,
Love,
Love,

Love.

*I stopped reaching
something in me
finally softened*

*Not into answers
but into
allowing*

*Surrender
was never the end*

ABOUT THE AUTHOR

Jaime Crowe is a writer and the creator of City Bathing, an urban immersion practice rooted in mindfulness, somatics, and compassionate noticing.

Her work explores grief, belonging, and the quiet ways we come back to ourselves in the midst of city life.

Based in New York City, she walks, wanders, notices, and writes, following the quiet call of the unknown.

Emptied is her first book.

The cover artwork was created by the author as a visual companion to the poems. An echo of what empties, circles, and quietly remains.